A Night At Phillies

Written by Tommy Watkins

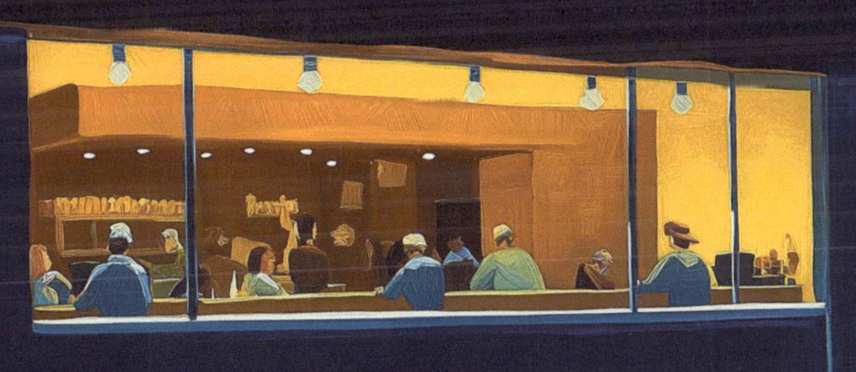

A man is sitting alone at a bar,

hoping a woman entering his life

would change everything.

He is a successful man.

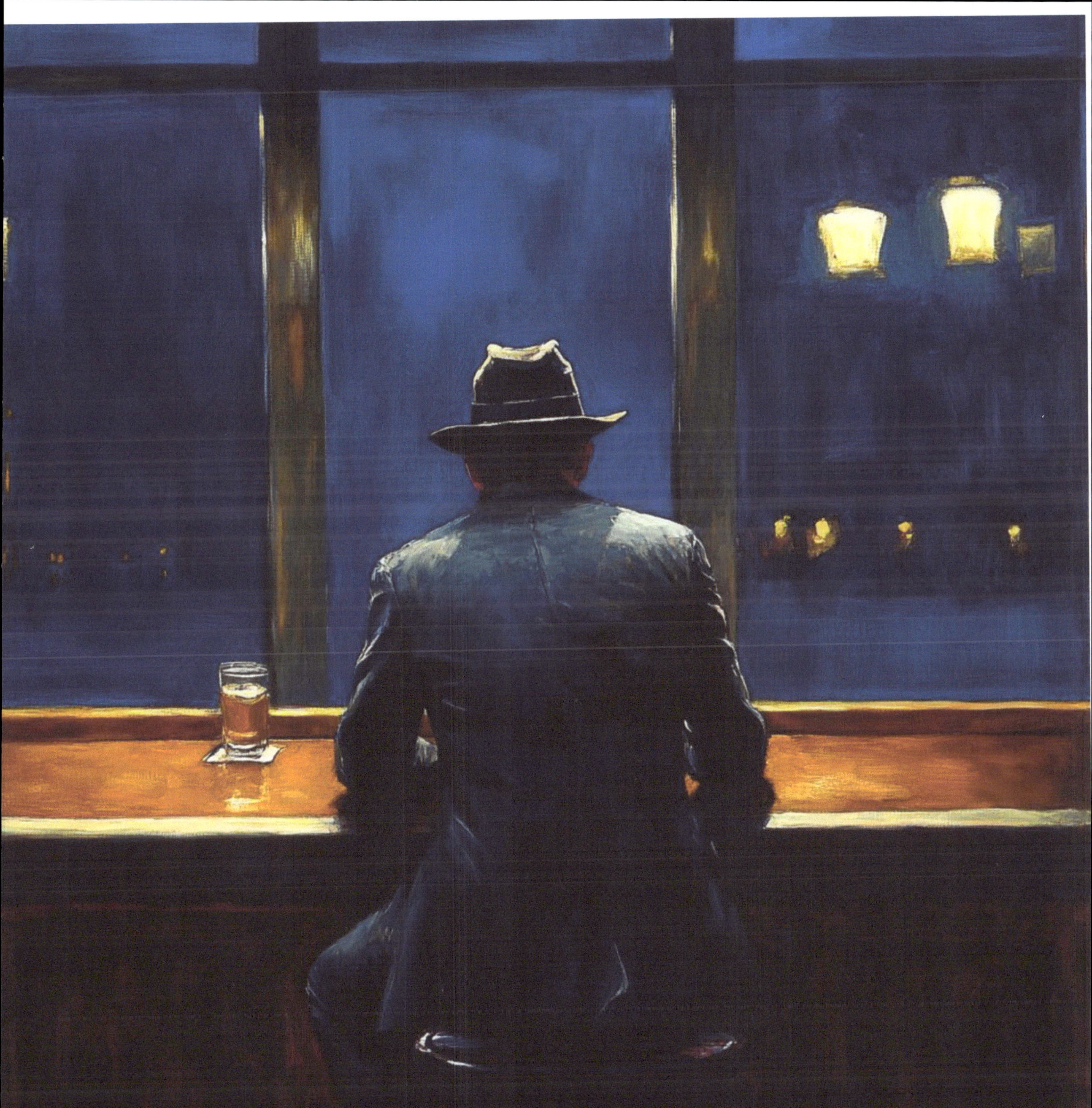

A husband and wife sit in a bar having drinks.

The couple couldn't be more opposite.

They don't say a word to each other

the entire night.

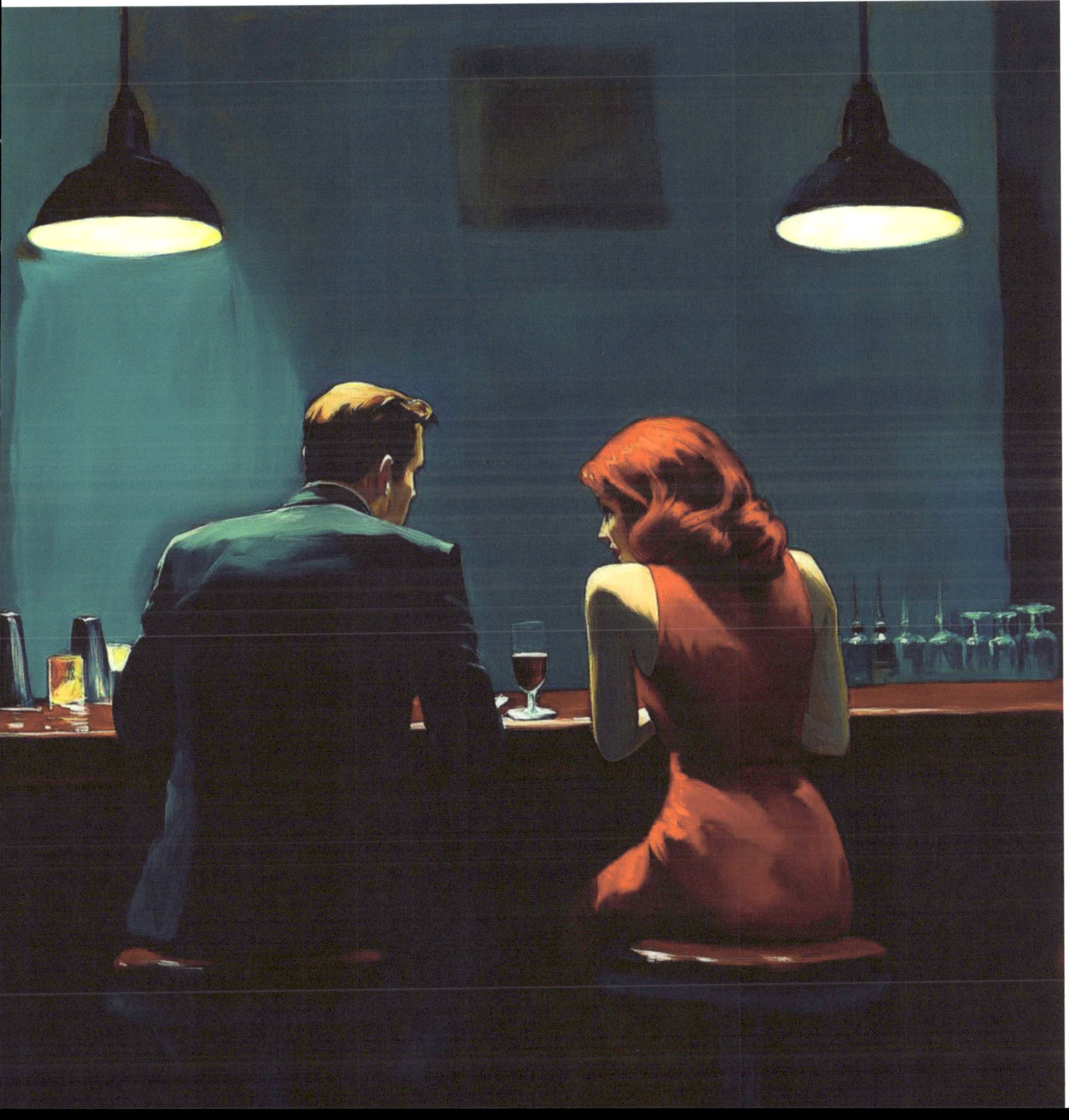

The bartender is ready to finish work.

These bartending hours are killing him.

He never gets to see his family.

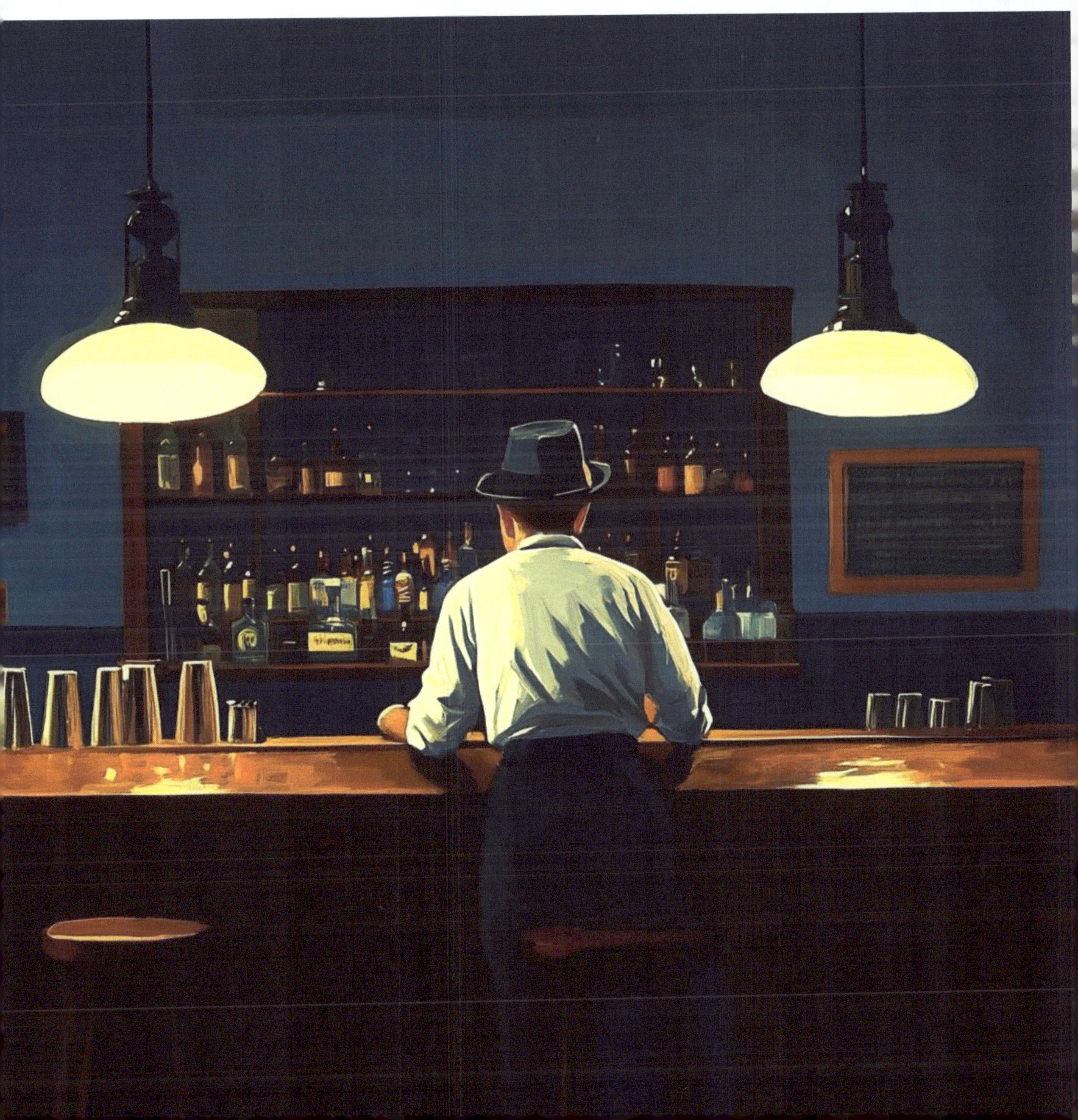

It's starting to be a wild night at Phillies.

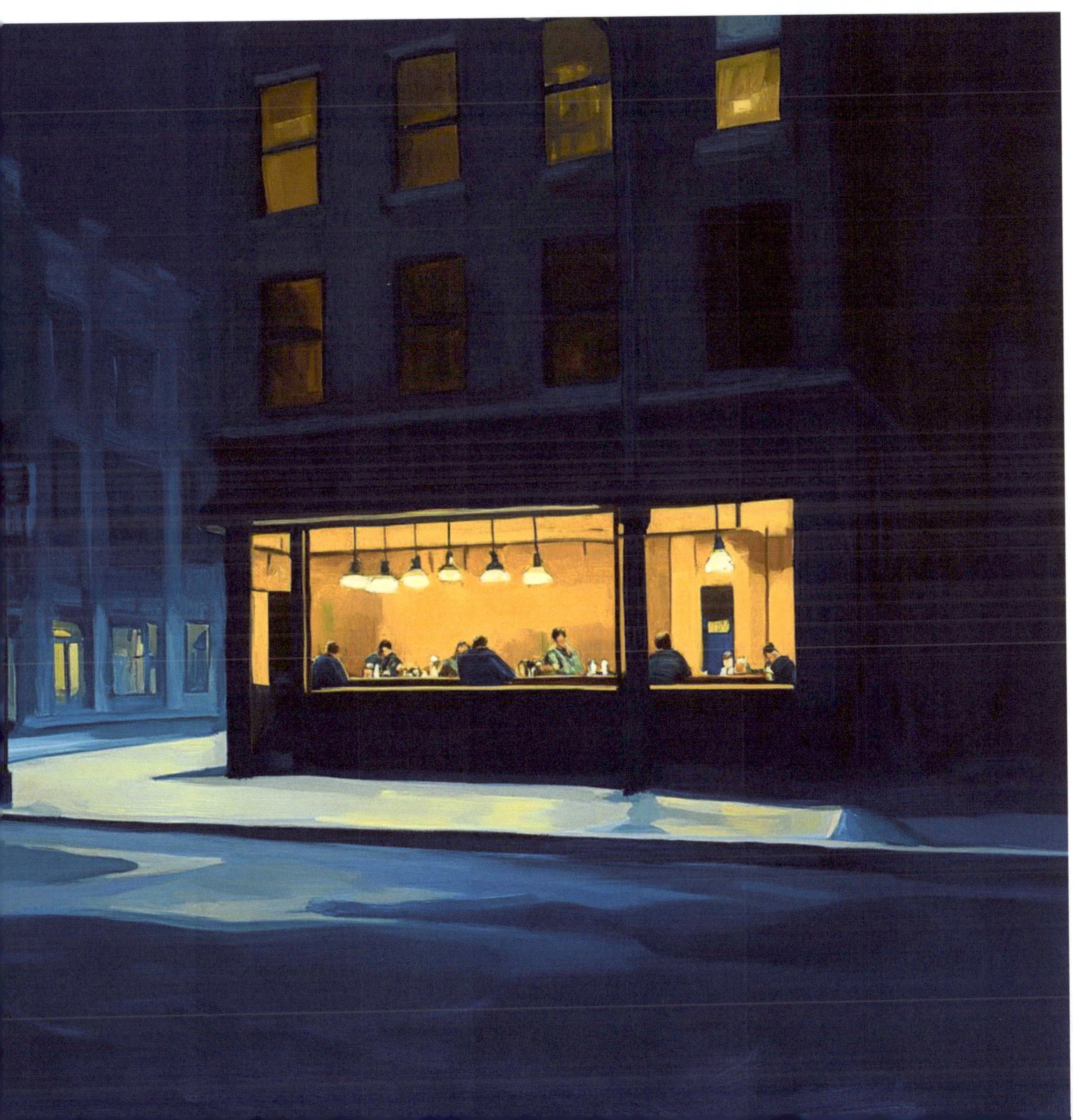

After a few drinks,

the couple gets into a huge fight.

They decide that night to get a divorce.

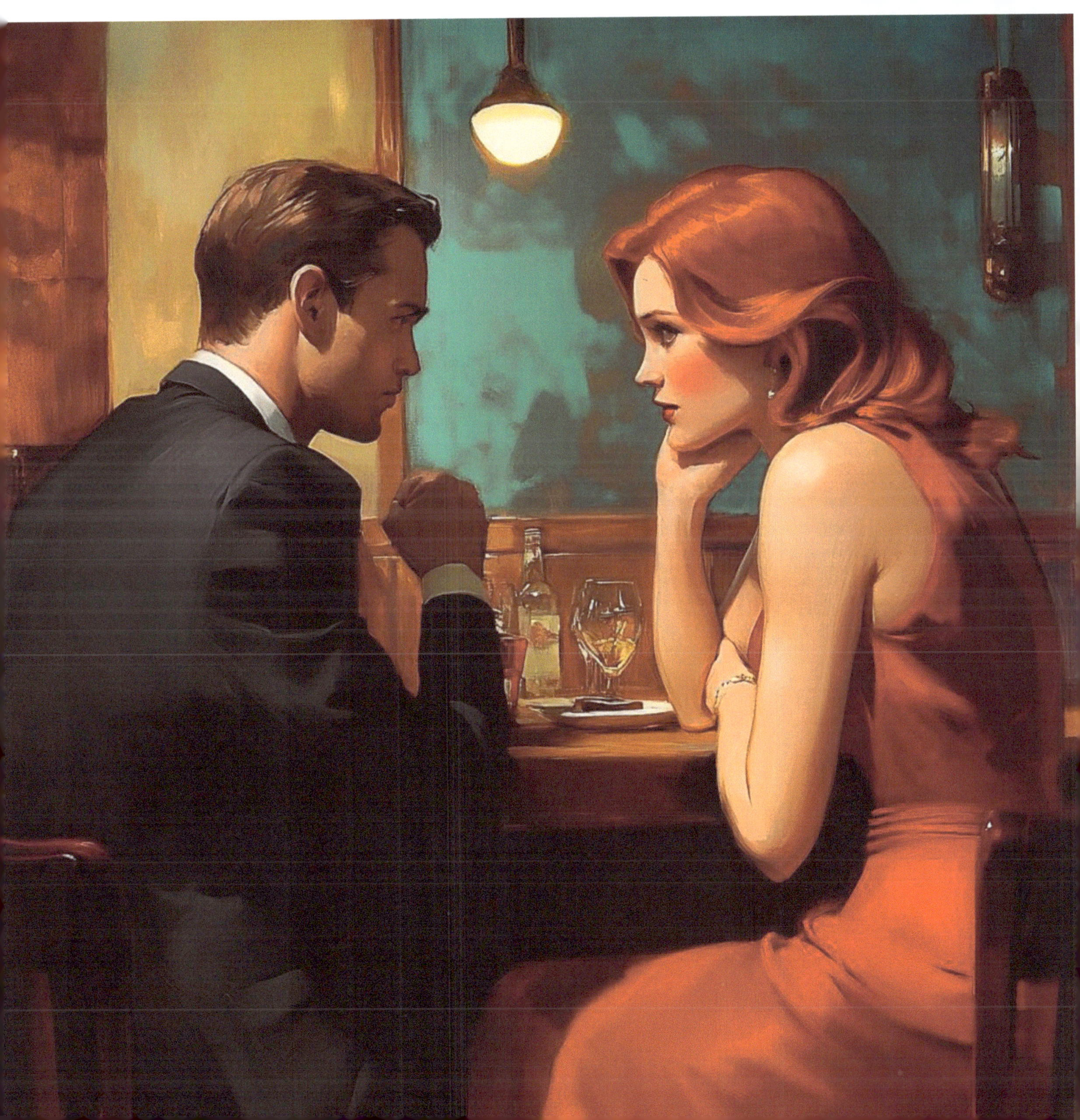

The rich man decides to swoop in

and flirt with the

newly separated wife.

He shows the wife how much money he has.

They drink too much and go home together.

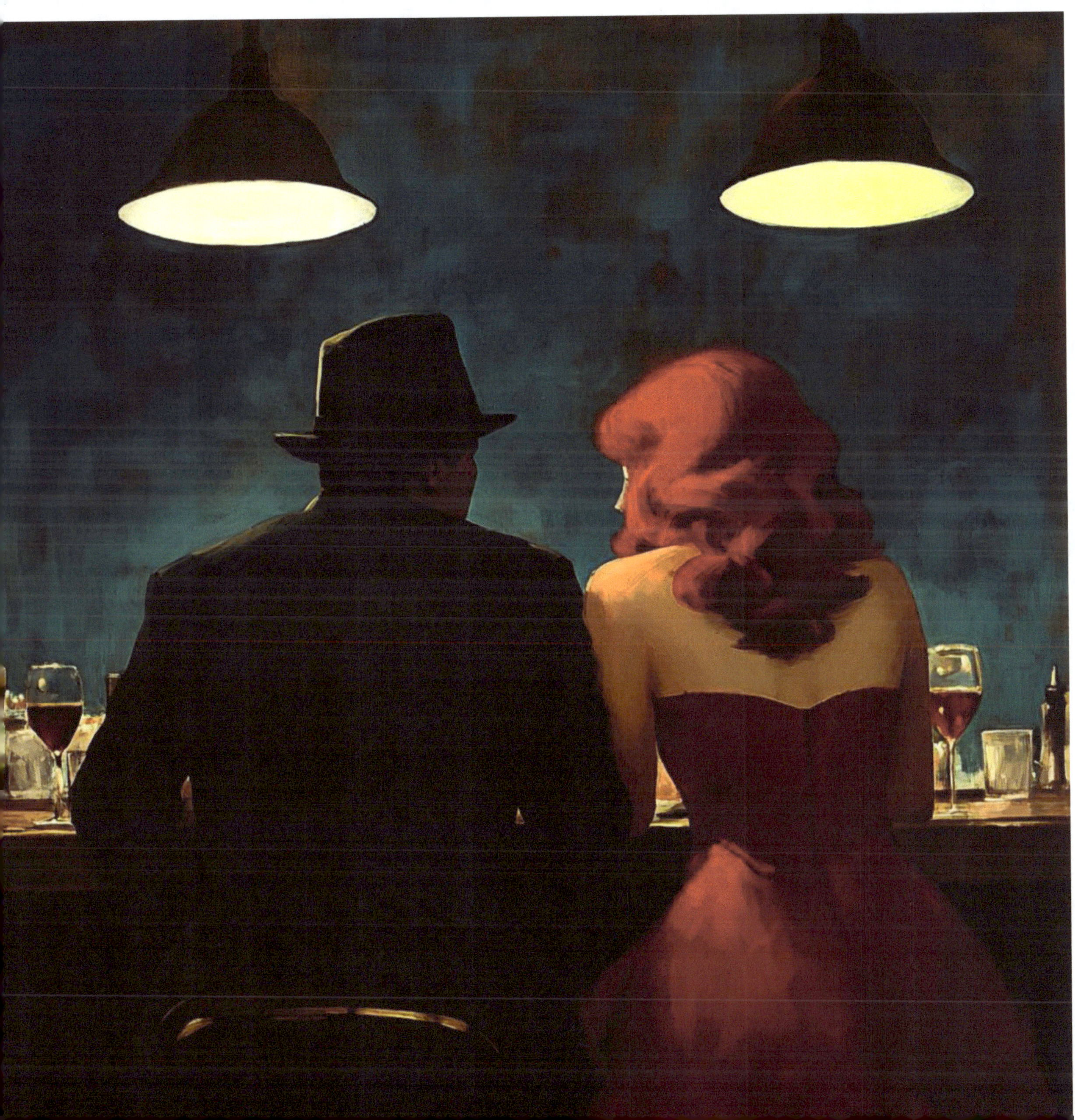

Looking at his watch,

the bartender gets angry.

He walks off his job and goes home.

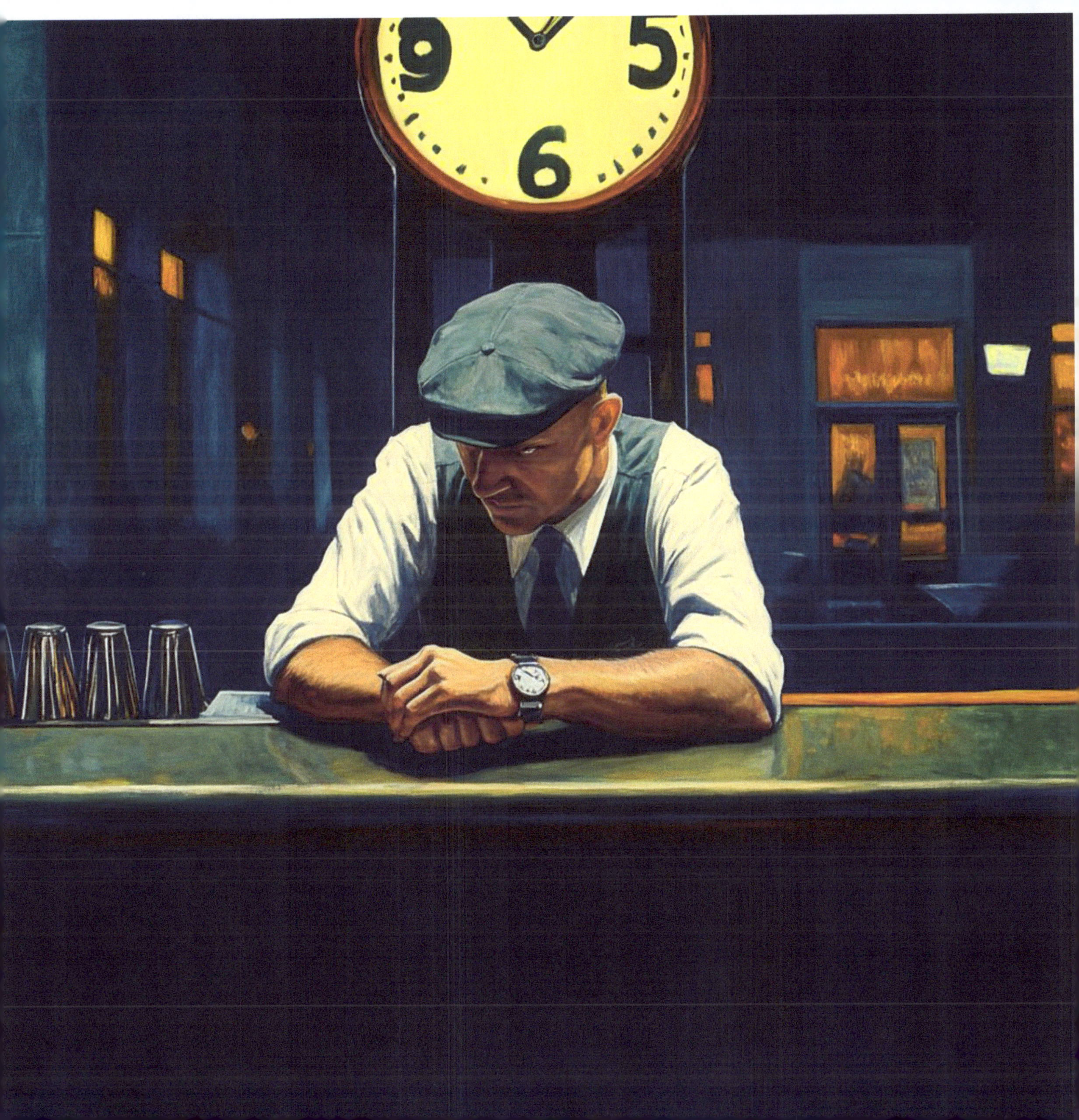

With no one to tend the bar,

the recently divorced

husband needs extra money

to support the cost of the divorce.

He jumps behind the bar

and starts bartending.

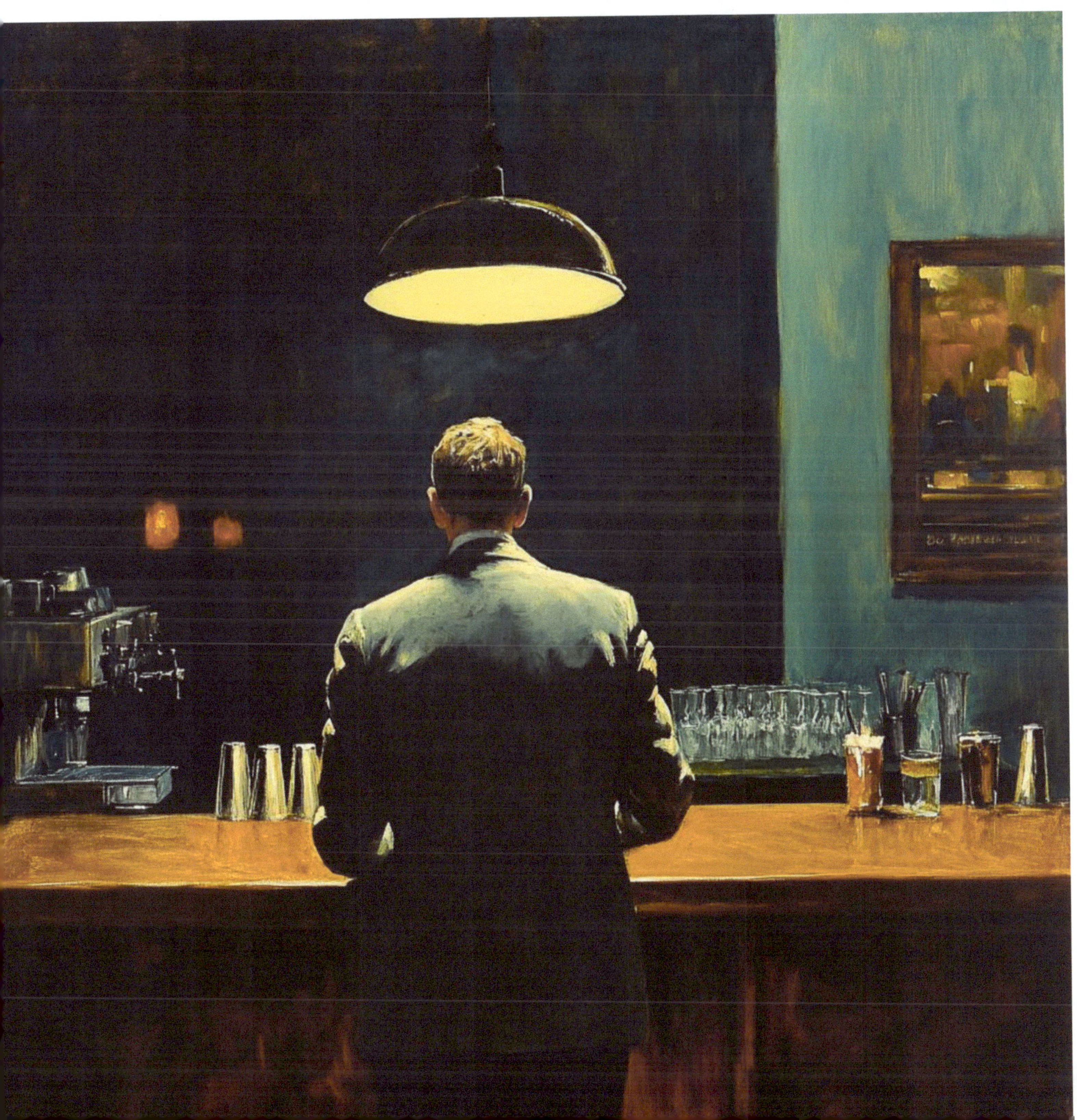

It was another wild night at Phillies Bar.

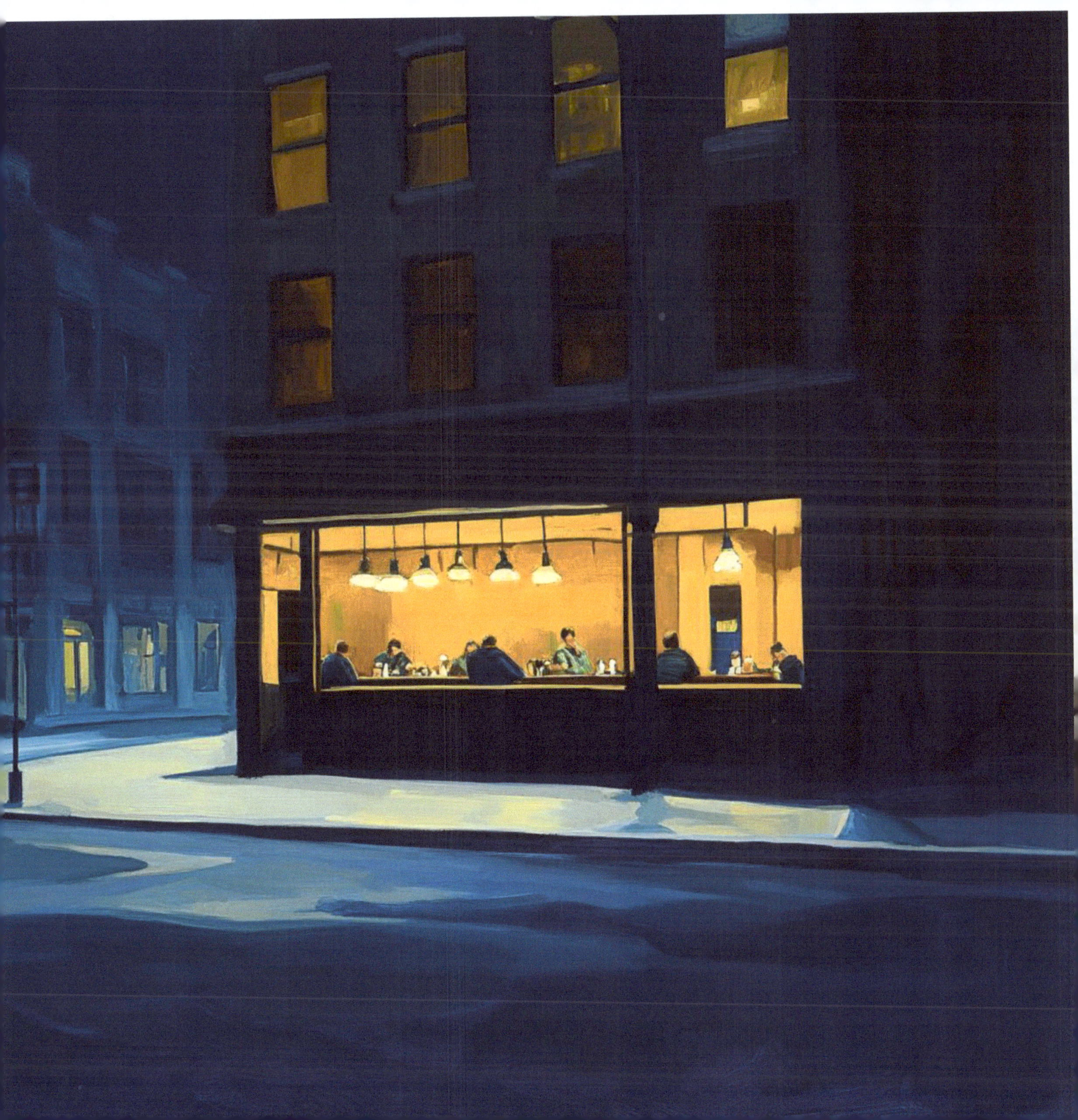

The End

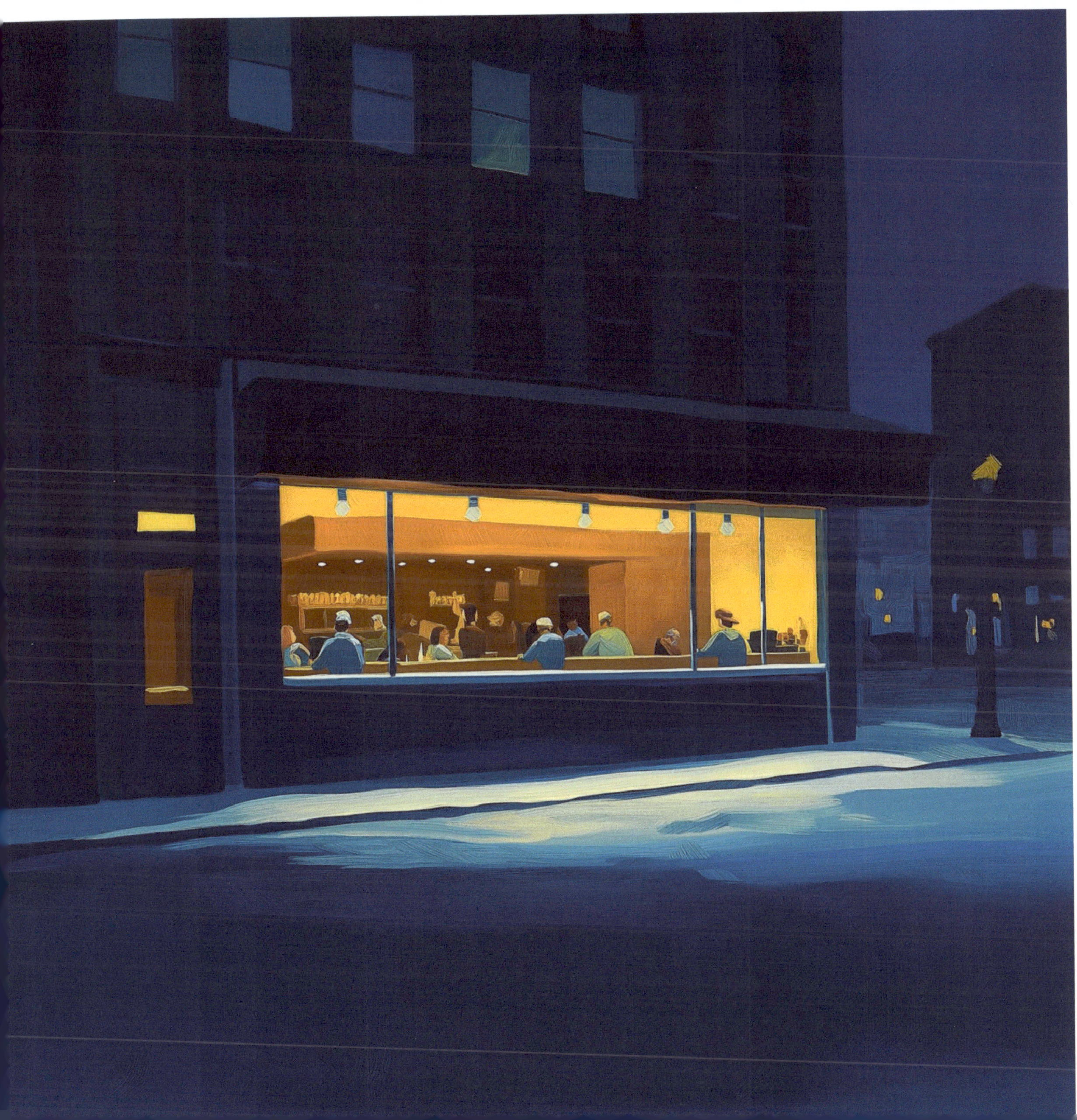